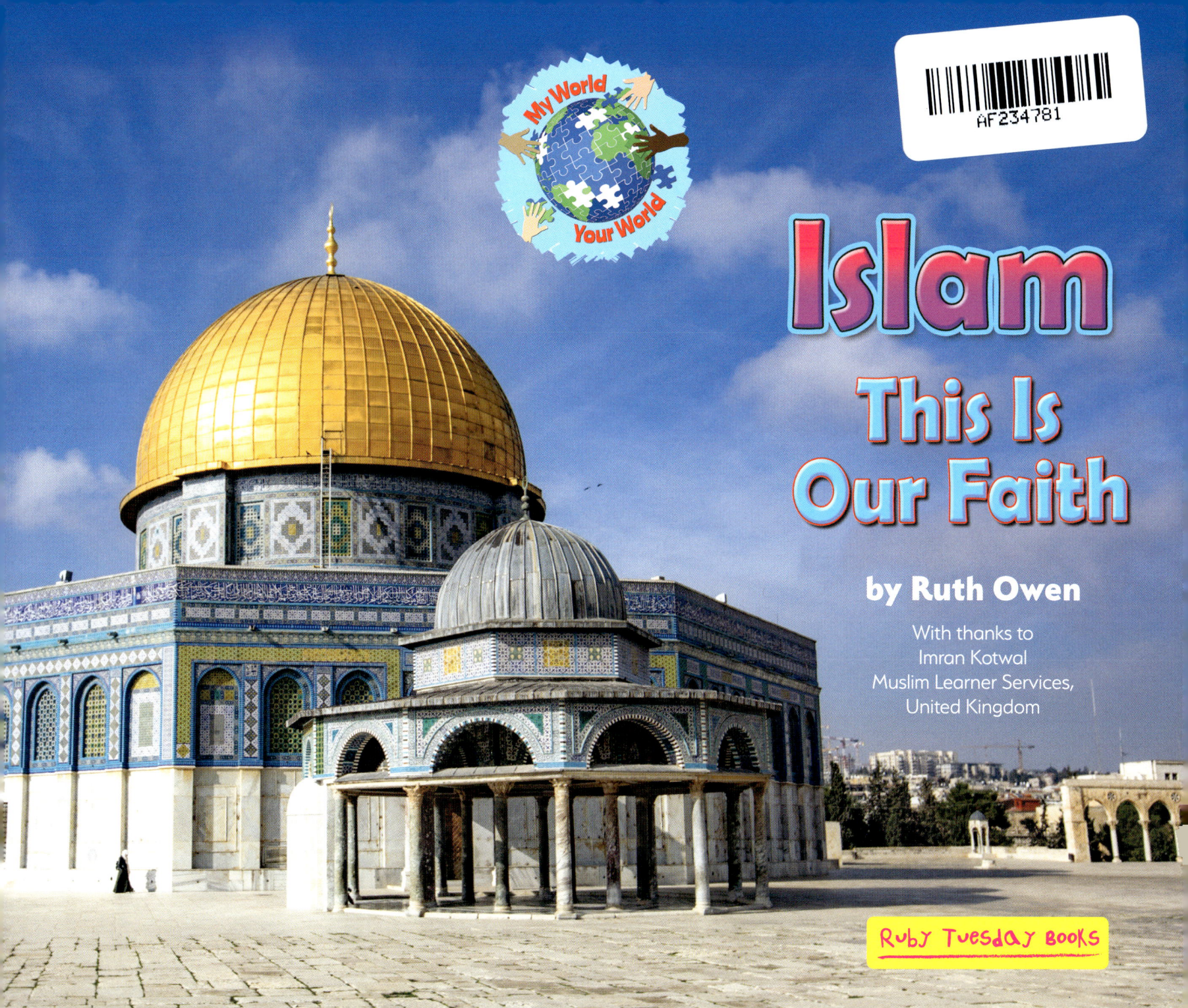

My World
Your World

Islam
This Is Our Faith

by Ruth Owen

With thanks to
Imran Kotwal
Muslim Learner Services,
United Kingdom

Ruby Tuesday Books

Published in 2026 by Ruby Tuesday Books Ltd.
Copyright © 2026 Ruby Tuesday Books Ltd.

Editor: Mark J. Sachner
Design & Production: Tammy West

Photo Credits:

Alamy: Cover (Louise Batalla Duran), 4 (Ellinnur Bakarudin), 7BL (Jim West), 10B (Athar Akram/MuslimPhotos.Net), 13R (Andi Muh Ridwan), 14 (Mahathir Mohd Yasin), 17B (Panther Media Global), 18B (Lee Thomas), 23L (David Grossman); Shutterstock: 1 (MWPhotos55), 2 (Kiri Photography), 5 (Sony Herdiana), 6 (Insight-Photography), 7TR (PeopleImages), 8 (India Picture), 9TL (parianto), 9BR (Muhammad ZA), 10T (Pixel-Shot), 11T (Odua Images), 11BR (New Africa/Fadhli Adnan), 12 (saiko3p), 13L (HU Art and Photography), 15TR (Augustine Bin Jumat), 15B (iamsevensix), 16 (Odua Images), 17T (MalikNalik), 18T (Hariyanto Surbakti), 19L (anythings), 19R (Fevziie), 20 (paulaphoto), 21 (irwan idris), 22 (ZouZou), 23R (Maharani afifah).

British Library Cataloguing in Publication Data (CIP) is available for this title.

ISBN 978-1-78856-212-6

Printed in Malta by Gutenberg Press

www.rubytuesdaybooks.com

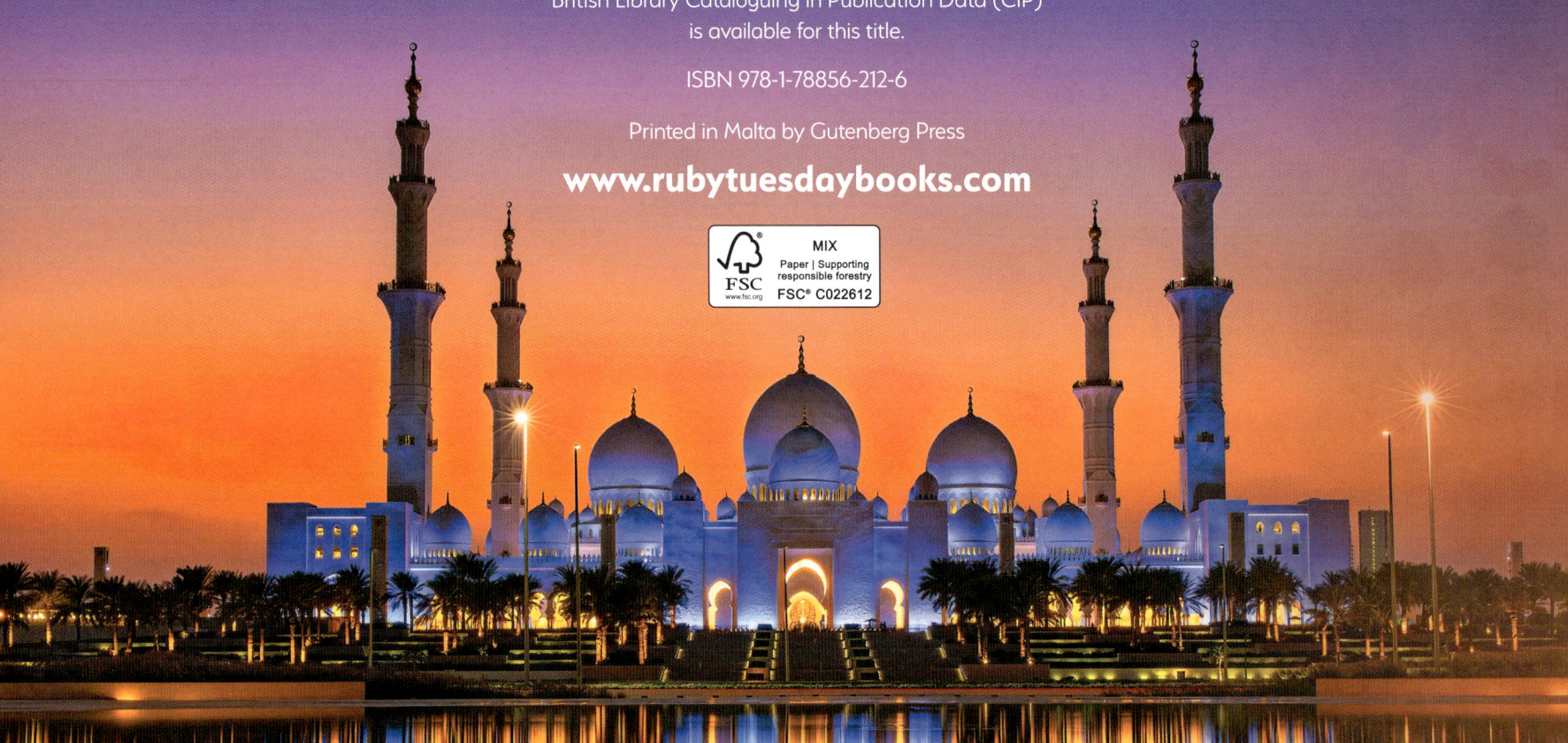

MIX
Paper | Supporting responsible forestry
FSC
www.fsc.org
FSC® C022612

Contents

**Words shown in bold in the text
are explained in the glossary.**

This Is Our Faith

Islam is a faith that began more than 1400 years ago.

People who follow this faith are called Muslims.

Muslims believe in one God, Allah, who created the universe and everything in it.

Muslims follow the teachings of the **Prophet** Muhammad.

Allah is the **Arabic** word for God.

This is how Allah is written in Arabic.

A Muslim family in Malaysia

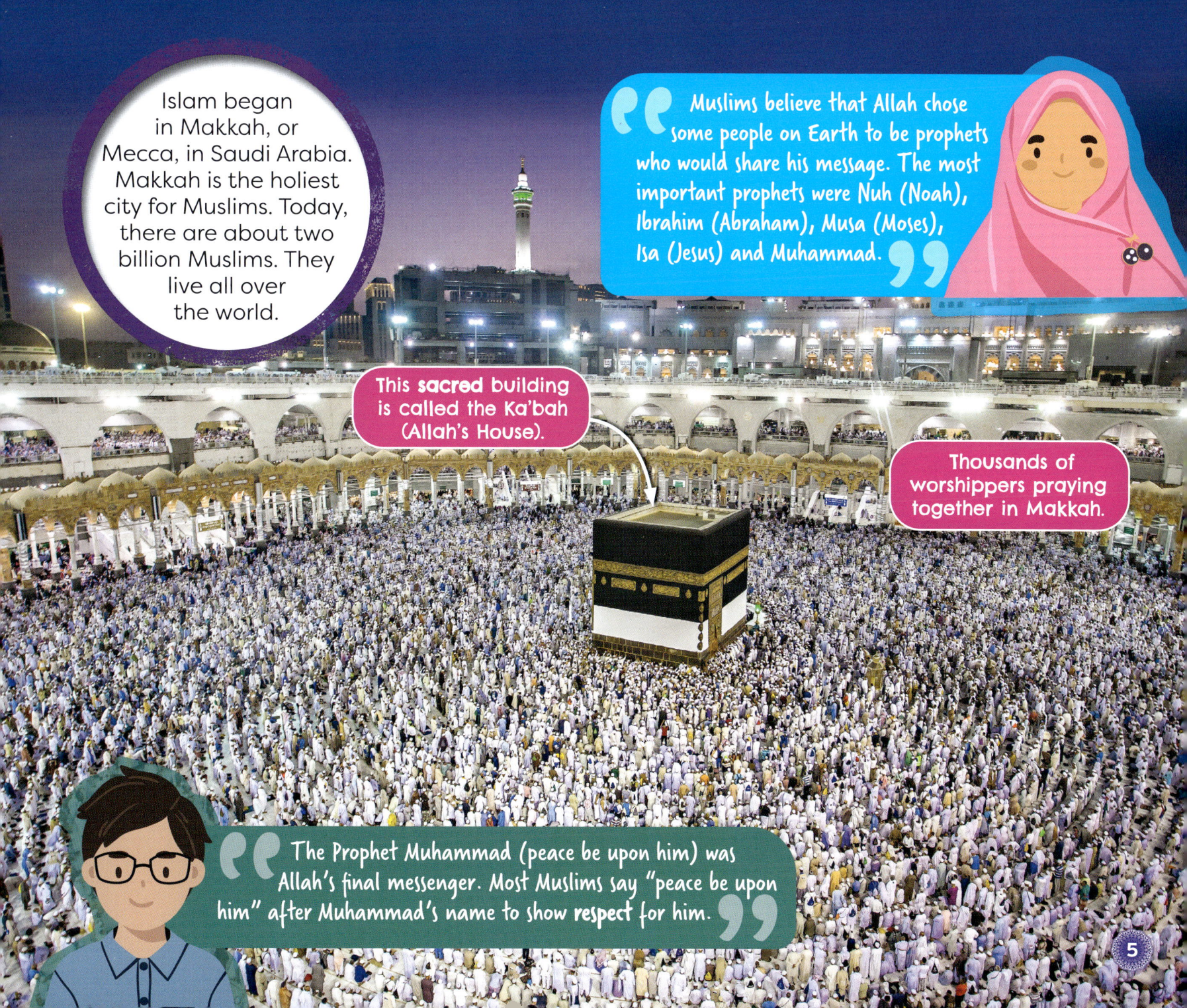

Islam began in Makkah, or Mecca, in Saudi Arabia. Makkah is the holiest city for Muslims. Today, there are about two billion Muslims. They live all over the world.

Muslims believe that Allah chose some people on Earth to be prophets who would share his message. The most important prophets were Nuh (Noah), Ibrahim (Abraham), Musa (Moses), Isa (Jesus) and Muhammad.

This **sacred** building is called the Ka'bah (Allah's House).

Thousands of worshippers praying together in Makkah.

The Prophet Muhammad (peace be upon him) was Allah's final messenger. Most Muslims say "peace be upon him" after Muhammad's name to show **respect** for him.

The Prophet Muhammad

The Prophet Muhammad was born in Makkah, or Mecca, around the year 570 CE.

Muslims believe that Allah sent the **Angel** Jibreel (Gabriel) to bring Allah's words to Muhammad.

Jibreel first came to Muhammad in the Cave of Hira. The cave is on Jabal al-Nour, the Mountain of Light, near Makkah.

Jabal al-Nour

People climbing the mountain to visit the cave

Muhammad began to tell people about Allah.

He taught that there is one God, Allah. He also taught people to be kind and caring.

> **Muslims try to follow the teachings of the Prophet Muhammad every day.**

We never hurt other people.

We don't steal or waste things.

We help those who are in need.

We show care and respect to others.

We always try to tell the truth.

We care about animals and nature.

Muslim families in the United States help pack donated food for families who don't have enough to eat.

> We can show kindness in many ways. I **donated** the toys I no longer play with to a **charity**. I made some sweets for my neighbour who was ill.

The Qur'an

The Muslim **holy** book is called the Qur'an.

Muslims believe it contains Allah's words that were brought to the Prophet Muhammad by the Angel Jibreel (Gabriel).

This girl is learning Arabic during an online lesson.

The Qur'an is written in Arabic. Most Muslims learn Arabic so they can read the Qur'an and pray in Arabic.

The Qur'an is always treated with respect.

Some Muslims keep their Qur'an wrapped in a special cloth or cover.

Most Muslims place the Qur'an on a high place to show respect to Allah's words.

Teacher

These children in Indonesia are studying the Qur'an at school.

The Qur'an

A Rehal

"Before touching the Qur'an, Muslims perform a special wash called Wudhu. Some Muslims may use a wooden stand, called a Rehal, when reading the Qur'an."

How We Worship

Muslims can pray in a **mosque** or at home. They can also pray in other places, such as at school or outdoors.

There are five daily prayers. This is called Salah.

Prayer times are dawn, after midday, late afternoon, sunset and at night.

A family praying at home

Before praying, Muslims perform a special wash called Wudhu.

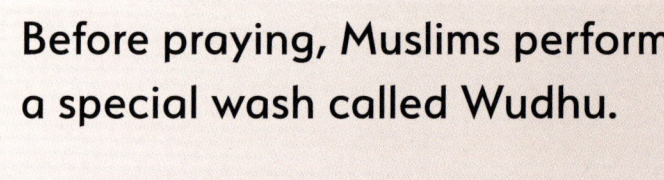

A family in Morocco doing Wudhu at a mosque before praying

When praying at home, Muslims usually have a prayer mat.

They stand on the mat and move through different prayer positions.

As I pray, I repeat the movements several times. I recite verses from the Qur'an and say "Allahu akbar" (Allah is great) many times.

Prayer mat

A compass on a phone App shows the direction of Makkah.

As they pray, Muslims all over the world face towards the sacred Ka'bah (Allah's House) in Makkah.

Welcome to a Mosque

A mosque, or masjid, is a building where Muslims come together to pray.

Friday is a holy day for Muslims. The most important prayer service at a mosque takes place at midday on Friday. This service is called Jumu'ah.

A tall tower called a minaret

A dome

A mosque in Tajikistan

When they go to a mosque, Muslims wear **modest** clothes to show respect. Women and girls cover their heads with a hijab. Some men and boys wear a cap called a kufi or topi.

People take off their shoes to enter the mosque.

If they haven't already performed Wudhu, they can wash at the mosque.

A prayer hall in a mosque

The mihrab

The imam

At a mosque, men and women may pray in different rooms, or different parts of the prayer hall.

Worshippers pray in the prayer hall. A person called an imam leads the prayers.

A special part of the wall, called the mihrab, shows the direction of prayer towards Makkah.

The Five Pillars of Islam

There are five important duties in Islam.

The duties are called the Five Pillars of Islam.

Every year, if they can afford to, Muslims must donate some money to charity. It is used to help the poor in their community and around the world.

THE FIVE PILLARS OF ISLAM

Shahadah
The belief in one God (Allah) and His messenger

Salah
Praying five times a day

Zakat
Giving money to charity

Sawm
Fasting during the month of Ramadan

Hajj
Making a **pilgrimage** to Makkah once in their lifetime

A man gives Zakat money at his mosque.

Every day I say, "There is no God but Allah, and Muhammad is His messenger." These important words are the Shahadah.

During Hajj, **pilgrims** visit sacred places in and around Makkah. They take part in different **rituals**.

One ritual is to walk around the Ka'bah seven times in an anticlockwise direction.

Many pilgrims wear white to show everyone is equal.

The Ka'bah is a large, cube-shaped structure.

Hajj is a special time for Muslims. They show their dedication to Allah, say sorry for past mistakes and make a fresh start in their lives.

Pilgrims performing Hajj

Muslims believe the Ka'bah (Allah's House) was built by the Prophet Ibrahim.

The Holy Month of Ramadan

A family reads the Qur'an during Ramadan

Muslims believe that the words of Allah were revealed to the Prophet Muhammad during Ramadan.

Ramadan is the ninth month of the **Muslim calendar**.

During Ramadan, Muslims fast between dawn and sunset. This is called sawm.

When fasting, Muslims are not allowed to eat or drink. Sometimes, older people, children or people who are unwell do not take part.

"During this holy month, Muslims spend more time praying and reading the Qur'an. They try to be extra kind, forgive others and give up bad habits.

Every evening, just after sunset, people break their fast.

They usually do this by eating some dates with a drink of water.

A family breaking fast

An iftar meal

Dates

A Muslim community in Turkey enjoying iftar outdoors

Then people eat the Ramadan evening meal, called iftar.

> " Fasting teaches us self-control. It helps us remember that many people are hungry and do not have enough to eat. "

Let's Celebrate! Eid ul-Fitr

Muslims mark the end of Ramadan with the festival of Eid ul-Fitr.

There is a special prayer on the day of Eid at mosques or outside at special Eid gatherings.

Eid ul-Fitr means "festival of breaking of the fast".

Eid prayers on a beach in Indonesia

Families celebrate at an Eid funfair in London.

We wish each other Eid Mubarak. It means "Happy Eid" or "Blessed Eid".

Eid ul-Fitr is a time for families to come together, celebrate and remember Allah.

A gift of money

Families and friends share special Eid ul-Fitr meals.

People may give presents and some families give money to children.

"During Eid, Muslims give money to charity to help others buy food and enjoy the celebrations. This money is called Zakat-ul-Fitr. I like to give some of my pocket money."

New Baby Celebrations

When a baby is born, the father usually whispers the words of the Adhan into the baby's ear.

Sometimes, another family member does this.

Father

The Adhan is called out from mosques to call people to pray.

The baby hears the name Allah from its first moments.

New baby

Most families cut the new baby's hair. The hair is weighed and then the same weight of silver or money is given to charity.

The new baby is named – often with a name that has a good meaning.

Many Muslim boys are given the name Muhammad to show love and respect for the prophet.

Cutting the new baby's hair

My name is Hana. It means "happiness". My brother is named Muhammad, which means "praised one".

Welcome to a Muslim Wedding

At a Muslim wedding, a ceremony called the Nikah unites the bride and groom.

Bride

Groom

A Muslim wedding in a mosque in the UK

The groom gives the bride a gift of money or jewellery called mahr.

The couple agree to marry and two people must **witness** the agreement.

The Nikah service is usually led by an imam.

After the Nikah there is a celebration feast called a walima.

A walima wedding feast in the United States.

Muslims come from many different countries and cultures. Sometimes, brides and grooms wear traditional clothes from their country or culture at their wedding.

The Prophet Muhammad encouraged Muslims to have a walima after marriage.

It is a way for the bride and groom to share their joy with family and friends.

An Indonesian bride and groom

GLOSSARY

angel
In Muslim beliefs, special winged beings made out of light – for example, the Angel Jibreel (Gabriel).

Arabic
A language spoken by people in the Middle East and parts of Africa. Some words in this book are Arabic, such as masjid (mosque).

charity
An organisation that collects money and uses it to help others. In Islam, Zakat is giving money to help others, such as people who do not have enough to eat.

donate
To give money, food or other goods to a charity.

fasting
In Islam, not eating or drinking between dawn and sunset during the month of Ramadan.

holy
Very special and important, and connected to God — for example, the holy Qur'an.

modest
Not too tight or short, or showing off too much of a person's body.

mosque
A building where Muslims gather to worship and spend time with their community.

Muslim calendar
A lunar calendar that uses the phases, or movements, of the Moon to organise the year into months. It is also called the Islamic calendar.

pilgrim
In Islam, a person who goes on a pilgrimage to Makkah (Mecca).

pilgrimage
For Muslims, a special journey to Makkah (Mecca) called Hajj. One of the five pillars of Islam.

prophet
A person chosen by God to be a messenger on Earth. Prophets share God's words and teachings with other people.

respect
Acting in a kind, careful and polite way to show that a person, place or belief is important to you.

ritual
A set of actions that are done in a certain order.

sacred
Something that is special or holy. It is usually important because it is connected to God.

witness
To see something happen.

INDEX